Alexisms

Useful Life Lessons from A
Recovering Serial Entrepreneur

By Alex Mandossian

For further inquiries , please email
support@MarketingOnlineFunnel.com

Heritage House International, Inc.
c/o Alex Mandossian
530 Alameda del Prado, Suite 399
Novato, CA 94949

First Printing: October 2015
Hardcover ISBN: 978-0-359-11812-0
Place of Publication: Silicon Valley, California, USA
Paperback Library of Congress Number: 2015951352

Trademarks

Warning and Disclaimer

Dedication

For the "Serial Entrepreneur" in you who
wants to live with honor by becoming the
person you pretend to be.

What I Do

I wake up, brush my teeth, and meditate in bed for fifteen minutes.

I workout at my gym for an hour, and when I get back home, I shower and then watch a TED talk while eating breakfast.

I put on some comfortable clothes, slide my indigo "Carpe Vitae" wristband over my right wrist, and hop in my car. I drive to Peet's Coffee, and during my fifteen-minute commute, I listen to a self-help CD.

When I arrive at Peet's, the barista, John, prepares what's arguably the best double wet cappuccino in North America. I surround myself with people, but I don't make any conversation. I don't check email or listen to voicemail messages while sipping my cappuccino.

For over an hour, I work fanatically, pounding on my MacBook Air keyboard with the intention to complete one of the three priorities I've set for the day. When my iPhone alarm rings, I power down my laptop and drive to my office, where I'll spend the rest of my day.

It's 9:30 a.m. now. I feel an exhilarating sense of productivity. How much have I produced? I don't care. Is the work I've produced any good? I don't spend energy thinking about it. What's most important is that I've "moved the needle" and I've focused on progress, not perfection, and that alone marks the difference in entrepreneurship.

When I pass through the front door of my office, I smile and secretly celebrate with a sense of cheerful expectancy for the rest of the day. I think to myself, "Wow, it's just 10 a.m., and I've already slayed the double-headed dragon of *procrastination and perfectionism!*"

As I sit at my desk ready to dive into my day, I'm reminded of my favorite *Alexism*: **"Sloppy success is better than perfect mediocrity."**

What I Know

There's a secret that high-performing Entrepreneurs know that low-performing entrepreneurs don't. It's a secret that can be expressed in two simple sentences. Here they are, so please read carefully:

> "Passion doesn't produce commitment.
> It's commitment that produces passion."

I read those words years go in a memo written by a mentor of mine, and I'm reminded of their meaning day after day. In nature and in business, first you need the wood, and then you get the fire. Think of *commitment* as the wood and *passion* as the fire.

In my 25+ years in business, I've met plenty of passionate business people who are miserable. I still know many who are passionate, but they're broke. And sadly, I even know a few who are passionately suicidal.

But to this day, I have yet to meet a *committed* entrepreneur who is any of those things. Commitment sparks passion. Commitment fuels passion. It's not the other way around. It's true that passion is critical for wild success, but without commitment, it's impotent.

If the passionate Abraham Lincoln lacked the commitment to deal with the ridicule of millions of Americans, he never would have had the courage to abolish slavery. If a passionate J.K. Rowling lacked the commitment of publishing her very first *Harry Potter*, despite the rejection of dozens of publishers, her six sequels would have never impacted hundreds of millions of kids and adults around the world.

It's commitment that produces passion. Passion does not produce commitment. Remember that as you read these *Alexisms*, especially when you face adversity in your next business deal. Commitment is the mortar that cements the bricks of your passions together. I hope you're committed to keep this handbook close by as a companion to lean on as you transition from one passion to the next.

What I Want

The book you hold in your hands is not original. I haven't created the life lessons you're about to read. But I have *curated* them into what I believe is a witty, wise, and even wacky compilation of ideals you can lean on. I like to review this *Alexisms* handbook before a speech, while writing an article, or when conducting any of my virtual trainings.

The *Alexisms* found in this handbook make me sound smarter.

It's true that the occasional inability to get started ("procrastination") and the tendency to never finish ("perfectionism") haunts and cripples the productivity of every entrepreneur I know. It's called "getting stuck." Whenever I feel stuck, I grab this book. It's full of random, yet useful ideas to get my mind moving again.

My hope is you'll utilize the following Alexisms in even more clever ways to get you unstuck with your business communications, and I hope you'll reach out to share those incidents with me on our private Facebook group: www.MarketingOnlineFunnel.com/MVPgroup Join us?

As I often think back to its origins, this handbook of *Alexisms* is a compendium of life lessons from 25+ years of experience in the Serial Entrepreneur world. Some *Alexisms* came from business breakthroughs, others from business challenges, and still others were key turning points in my professional and personal life.

I hope as you read these "slice-of-life" vignettes is that you read them again and again. They are ideal to share with your friends and colleagues on Twitter, Facebook, LinkedIn, Google+, or your favorite blogs. My deepest wish in sharing these Alexisms is that you'll find them rich with insight and enough flair to spark new social conversations and seeds of social influence.

Friend, I do hope our paths cross often!

Take the 4-minute Serial Entrepreneur Assessment at
MarketingOnlineFunnel.com

Contents

Take the 4-minute Serial Entrepreneur Assessment at

MarketingOnlineFunnel.com

Section I

Be Your Own Boss

Do you have what it takes to be your own boss?
Alex Mandossian share his views,
pointers, and resources on how to be a
successful entrepreneur.

1

You don't have to be a business hero to act like one.
@AlexMandossian

_____

_____

_____

2

Adrenaline is the breakfast of high achievers in entrepreneurship.
@AlexMandossian

_____

_____

_____

3

High-achieving entrepreneurs know that "well done is always better than well said."
@AlexMandossian

_____

_____

_____

4

What makes a good entrepreneur great is their uncanny ability to manage uncertainty.
@AlexMandossian

_____

_____

_____

5

Beware the evil twins of entrepreneurship:
1) Procrastination (Fear of "Starting")&
2) Perfectionism (Fear of Finishing)
@AlexMandossian

_____

_____

_____

6

Serial Entrepreneurs know that "action" is the
"doing" part of thinking.
@AlexMandossian

_____

_____

_____

7

Entrepreneurship is like skydiving. You don't
need a parachute to skydive, you just need a
parachute to skydive more than once."
@AlexMandossian

_____

_____

_____

8

The most terrifying feeling any entrepreneur
can have is to live into to fulfilling their "default"
future.
@AlexMandossian

_____

_____

_____

9

There's no such thing as a self-made success.
Every entrepreneur needs a mentor to find their
path to wild success.
@AlexMandossian

_____

_____

_____

10

The most important mindset a wildly successful
entrepreneur can have is "relaxed intensity."
@AlexMandossian

_____

_____

_____

11

There are 2 types of problems entrepreneurs face
each day: 1) Problem you currently have; and, 2)
Problem you will have!
@AlexMandossian

_____

_____

_____

12

When entrepreneurs pray, they speak to their
Inner Power. When they meditate, they listen to
their Inner Power.
@AlexMandossian

_____

_____

_____

13

Serial Entrepreneurs spend their imagination, not just their money.
@AlexMandossian

_____

_____

_____

14

Good entrepreneurs are "problem solvers".
Great entrepreneurs are "problem finder".
@AlexMandossian

_____

_____

_____

15

Great entrepreneurs teach their team members
and suppliers HOW to think, not WHAT to
think.
@AlexMandossian

_____

_____

_____

16

The 3 responsibilities of business leaders:
1) Define reality.
2) Protect confidences.
3) Communicate compassionately.
@AlexMandossian

_____

_____

_____

17

What makes a good entrepreneur great is to
THINK BIG and act small.
@AlexMandossian

_____

_____

_____

18

The secret to wild success in business is to be
willing to look bad in public more often than
your competitors.
@AlexMandossian

_____

_____

_____

19

It doesn't pay to be the type of entrepreneur who makes the same New Year's resolutions more than once.
@AlexMandossian

_____

_____

_____

20

Wildly successful business owners focus more on progress instead of perfection.
@AlexMandossian

_____

_____

_____

21

Social influence is permission-based.
"Command - and -control " managers
have been replaced by "engage -and-
enroll" leaders.
@AlexMandossian

_____

_____

_____

22

Effective "social influencers " are like the wind :
You can't see them, but you notice their presence.
@AlexMandossian

_____

_____

_____

23

Humility is the bedrock of servant leadership .
Aim to become the greatest business leader the
world has NEVER known.
@AlexMandossian

_____

_____

_____

24

Wildly successful entrepreneurs don't burst
through their comfort zones, they EXPAND their
comfort zones!
@AlexMandossian

_____

_____

_____

25

Social influencers who have the most relationship capital have figured out how to separate the people who dislike them from the people who are still undecided.
@AlexMandossian

_____

_____

_____

26

Business leaders who know, but don't do, still don't know!
@AlexMandossian

_____

_____

_____

27

High achievers know that take time it is better to "amplify less" than to "rush through more".
@AlexMandossian

_____

_____

_____

28

"Doubling down" is the high-achieving entrepreneur's marketingmantra.
@AlexMandossian

_____

_____

_____

29

Truly committed entrepreneurs re-invent their own economy.
@AlexMandossian

_____

_____

_____

30

Serial Entrepreneurs have the unique ability to be "creative ", which is nothing more than "the truth made fascinating."
@AlexMandossian

_____

_____

_____

31

The two -word definition of the ideal entrepreneurial mindset is: "Delayed Gratification."
@AlexMandossian

_____

_____

_____

32

Serial Entrepreneurs succeed by working in the trenches. It's easy to be brave from a distance.
@AlexMandossian

_____

_____

_____

33

Three things business owners can't take back:
1) A broken promise,
2) A neglected opportunity &
3) A day wasted.
@AlexMandossian

_____

_____

_____

34

Wildly successful entrepreneurs don't wait for
their "ship to come in," they "swim out to it!".
@AlexMandossian

_____

_____

_____

35

Entrepreneurial leaders don't just look for business heroes - they become one. @AlexMandossian

_____

_____

_____

Take the 4-minute Serial Entrepreneur Assessment at

MarketingOnlineFunnel.com

Section II

Take the First Step

Your business intentions are more important
than your business strategies. First, "What?"
then, "How?" This section will help you
transform your idea into a revenue-
generating venture.

36

The two most important days in your life is:
1) The day you were born , and 2) The day
you find out why.
@AlexMandossian

_____

_____

_____

37

No business "process" can exist until it's given
a name to define it.
@AlexMandossian

_____

_____

_____

38

During the "start-up" phase of any business, there's no such thing as a "little mistake."
@AlexMandossian

_____

_____

_____

39

In any business start-up, remember that "pain is inevitable, but suffering is optional."
@AlexMandossian

_____

_____

_____

40

Premise must precede purpose in business. The former asks, "What do I believe?" The latter asks, "Why do I believe it?"
@AlexMandossian

_____

_____

_____

41

The difference between an amateur and a professional in any business venture- making is the first dollar earned.
@AlexMandossian

_____

_____

_____

42

The first step in growing any business is to define reality. The second step is to accept it! @AlexMandossian

_____

_____

_____

43

Business growth opportunities can be divided into two areas:
1) What matters most &
2) Everything else.
@AlexMandossian

_____

_____

_____

44

The mindset that separates you from others in business is to treat your relationship capital with "unlimited liability."
@AlexMandossian

_____

_____

_____

45

When growing your business, it's possible to get "anything" you want, but not always "everything" you want.
@AlexMandossian

_____

_____

_____

46

The only thing worse than going the wrong direction in business is going the wrong direction enthusiastically!
@AlexMandossian

_____

_____

_____

47

When growing a "service business," the best strategy is to sacrifice short-term profits in exchange for long-term wealth.
@AlexMandossian

_____

_____

_____

48

It's better to create a company out of a great Unique Selling Proposition (USP) than to create a great USP out of a company.
@AlexMandossian

_____

_____

_____

49

It is better to grow deep roots before picking ripe fruits. Build your business like a bamboo plant, not a eucalyptus tree.
@AlexMandossian

_____

_____

_____

Take the 4-minute Serial Entrepreneur Assessment at
MarketingOnlineFunnel.com

Section III

Attract a Great Team

"Together, Everyone Achieves More." A team with an outstanding business culture, plus the right skills, attitude, and commitment to back you up, is a great factor to a successful business venture.

50

Dropping the baton is not as crippling to a business team as the unwillingness to pass the baton.
@AlexMandossian

_____

_____

_____

51

If you're a true business leader, you've completed your job when your followers say, "We did it ourselves!"
@AlexMandossian

_____

_____

_____

52

When building your business team, remember that no one alone is smarter than everyone together.
@AlexMandossian

_____

_____

_____

53

Do an emotional MRI on every person you want to hire to join your team.
@AlexMandossian

_____

_____

_____

54

When vetting new team members, hire them for "attitude" and train them for "skills."
@AlexMandossian

_____

_____

_____

55

Everything is a mirror in your business. Remember that whenever you complain about a disloyal team member.
@AlexMandossian

_____

_____

_____

56

Business teams who "get along" typically outper-
form teams made up of high achievers. A great
culture trumps great talent.
@AlexMandossian

_____

_____

_____

57

Experienced high-achievers know that passion
doesn't produce commitment; commitment produces passion.
@AlexMandossian

_____

_____

_____

58

Bridging the gap between your vision and execution is the root of all business leadership.
@AlexMandossian

_____

_____

_____

59

Hiring a business mentor shaves off years of tri-al-and-error, because you can't read a label from inside the jar.
@AlexMandossian

_____

_____

_____

60

Delegating a Vision is a mistake. It's like giving up your newborn baby to an orphanage.
@AlexMandossian

_____

_____

_____

61

In business, when more than one person is held accountable, in reality, no one is!
@AlexMandossian

_____

_____

_____

62

Business meetings have 3 primary agendas:
1) Where you were,
2) Where you are, and
3) Where you're going.
@AlexMandossian

_____

_____

_____

63

The root issue to any business problem seems to always stem back to a human being.

_____

@AlexMandossian

_____

_____

64

When you build an ENGAGED business culture, it's much like "going to heaven without the inconvenience of dying."
@AlexMandossian

_____

_____

_____

Take the 4-minute Serial Entrepreneur Assessment at
MarketingOnlineFunnel.com

Section IV

Road to Success

Delayed gratification is the epitome of success in business. No business is successful on day one. The road to success in business is hardly the easy one. There may be obstacles on the way, but turning these obstacles into opportunities are the defining moments you'll remember most.

65

Sloppy success is better than perfect mediocrity.
@AlexMandossian

_____

_____

_____

66

There's no scarcity problem in business. It's a dis-
tribution problem of matching the right message
with the right market.
@AlexMandossian

_____

_____

_____

67

Whenever you want to dissolve a roadblock in
business, remember: "Seeing is not believing. Be
- lieving is seeing."
@AlexMandossian

_____

_____

_____

68

Never underestimate the power of denial when
you ask your business partners to admit their
mistakes.
@AlexMandossian

_____

_____

_____

69

Wild success in business is nothing more than ordinary tasks done consistently that produce extraordinary results.
@AlexMandossian

_____

_____

_____

70

The "Principle of Priority" is to know the difference between what's important and what's urgent ... and then to do what's urgent first!
@AlexMandossian

_____

_____

_____

71

The biggest reason for failure in business is to pay attention and avoid your daily distractions.
@AlexMandossian

_____

_____

_____

72

The single most important thing to do each business day is the single most important thing.
@AlexMandossian

_____

_____

_____

73

Spectacular achievement is always preceded by unspectacular planning for wildly successful Se- rial Entrepreneurs.
@AlexMandossian

_____

_____

_____

74

High achievement in business means to conduct business with a level of "high intention and low attachment."
@AlexMandossian

_____

_____

_____

75

Business "systems" can grow your profits; business "sequencing" can accelerate your wealth.
@AlexMandossian

_____

_____

_____

76

Never confuse activity with accomplishment. Which pilot do you trust more : The one who loves to fly or the one who loves to land?
@AlexMandossian

_____

_____

_____

77

There are 2 types of career regret:
1) Risks you took that didn't work, and
2) Risks you didn't take that could have.
@AlexMandossian

78

Saying "later" or "never" to new business projects
is far less decisive than saying, "Not now!"
@AlexMandossian

79

The risk of the wrong decision trumps the terror
of indecision in any business predicament.
@AlexMandossian

_____

_____

_____

80

High-achievers know that risk-taking is natural.
No one refuses to eat when hungry just because
of the risk of choking.
@AlexMandossian

_____

_____

_____

81

Unlearning a bad business habit is more difficult than learning a good business habit.
@AlexMandossian

_____

_____

_____

82

The greatest way to live with honor when grow-ing your business is to become the person you pretend to be.
@AlexMandossian

_____

_____

_____

83

Turning business obstacles into opportunities
are the defining moments you'll remember most.
@AlexMandossian

_____

_____

_____

84

Quantification is key to business success because
you can't improve what you don't measure.
@AlexMandossian

_____

_____

_____

85

Success in business is binary: You're either a
VICTIM or a VOLUNTEER.
@AlexMandossian

_____

_____

_____

86

Your biggest business headaches of today were
once your brightest ideas of yesterday. Own them,
and move onward and upward!
@AlexMandossian

_____

_____

_____

87

Gambling with your time to grow your business is silly, because unlike money, you're placing a bet you can'tcover.
@AlexMandossian

_____

_____

_____

88

Your unconditional guarantee attached to your offerings is an opportunity to resolve unspoken predicaments in your industry.
@AlexMandossian

_____

_____

_____

89

Clarity is the "sweet-spot" between expectation and direction in understanding the purpose of your business.
@AlexMandossian

_____

_____

_____

90

The quality of a good business answer is determined by the clarity of a great business question.
@AlexMandossian

_____

_____

_____

91

If you want to be hyper-productive in your business, make "No" your default answer to bright, shiny opportunities.
@AlexMandossian

_____

_____

_____

92

An entrepreneur without "Vision" is like an
Admiral who attempts to navigate a ship
without a rudder.
@AlexMandossian

_____

_____

_____

93

The key to managing uncertainty when growing your business is to never take yourself or your business too seriously.
@AlexMandossian

Take the 4-minute Serial Entrepreneur Assessment at
MarketingOnlineFunnel.com

Section V

Become a High-Achiever

Being successful is the easy part, but staying successful is a different story. Improving your business process with lesser cost while providing the same output is the challenge.

94

Your best client today was once a stranger, so if you want life-long clients, don't treat them like strangers.
@AlexMandossian

95

Something terrible happens when you don't engage prospects to become long-term buyers: NOTHING!
@AlexMandossian

96

Caring is the ultimate competitive advantage in starting and maintaining any business today.
@AlexMandossian

_____

_____

_____

97

Relationship capital is your most precious asset. We're no longer in the Information Age; rather, we are in the "Recommendation Age".
@AlexMandossian

_____

_____

_____

98

It pays to polarize prospects. They'll either "turn up the volume" or "change the channel" with your marketing messages.
@AlexMandossian

99

Public opinion always lags behind private reality.
@AlexMandossian

100

Focus on building momentum, not only growth.
It's better to aim for first-downs, not just touch-
downs.
@AlexMandossian

_____

_____

_____

101

Creating a sustainable cash-flow in business is to
first spend your imagination, not just your money.
@AlexMandossian

_____

_____

_____

102

Every business is a marketing business.
@AlexMandossian

_____

_____

_____

103

Sincerity in business means you eat your own
cooking and drink your own Kool-Aid. Remember that behavior never lies.
@AlexMandossian

_____

_____

_____

104

No major business predicament was ever re-
solved by unanimous consent.
@AlexMandossian

_____

_____

_____

105

Being trustworthy is neither good nor bad. It simply means you're acknowledged as being consis-
tent and predictable.
@AlexMandossian

_____

_____

_____

106

The most critically important question any business owner can ask: "What marketing idea are we testing today?"
@AlexMandossian

_____

_____

_____

107

Your prospects secretly ask three questions before buying: "Why this? Why you? Why now?"
@AlexMandossian

_____

_____

_____

108

A "beginner's mind" in business means you ac-
knowledge the fact that you're never the smartest
person in theroom.
@AlexMandossian

_____

_____

_____

109

To convince a new client to give you a BIG order,
look them in the eye and say, "I'm your 911."
@AlexMandossian

_____

_____

_____

110

Don't just launch a new product or service, create
a marketing movement!
@AlexMandossian

_____

_____

_____

111

True growth demands to temporarily sacrifice
your security.
@AlexMandossian

_____

_____

_____

112

All clients are created equal, but not all clients are treated equal. You must know which clients "butter" your daily bread.
@AlexMandossian

_____

_____

_____

113

Indifference to a client's needs is the greatest tragedy when growing any business.
@AlexMandossian

_____

_____

_____

114

If you want to keep your clients for life, give them value worthy of their devotion.
@AlexMandossian

_____

_____

_____

115

Fuzzy marketing targets never get hit.
@AlexMandossian

_____

_____

_____

116

The cost of doing the same thing without getting
different results is higher than the risk of making
permanent change.
@AlexMandossian

_____

_____

_____

Take the 4-minute Serial Entrepreneur Assessment at
MarketingOnlineFunnel.com

Section VI

Points to Ponder

Everyone needs an inspiration, and this list of phrases will supply you with something to reflect on to be a successful entrepreneur.

117

A definitive "No" to a business proposal is better than a "Maybe" without execution. @AlexMandossian

_____

_____

_____

118

The shortest distance between two points is not a straight line, it's the path of least resistance. @AlexMandossian

_____

_____

_____

119

Stealing winning ideas from one source is called "plagiarism," but borrowing from many sources is called "research."
@AlexMandossian

_____

_____

_____

120

Action is the antidote to ignorance. Not knowing what you don't know is not as tragic as not doing what you doknow.
@AlexMandossian

_____

_____

_____

121

Your daily DON'T DO list is more important than
your TO DO list.
@AlexMandossian

_____

_____

_____

122

Seek wisdom, not just knowledge. Knowledge is
knowing a tomato is a fruit; wisdom is not putting
tomatoes in fruit salad!
@AlexMandossian

_____

_____

_____

123

Entrepreneurial bravery is physical. Courage is mental. Boldness is emotional. And humility is spiritual. Go "4 for 4!"
@AlexMandossian

_____

_____

_____

124

Your professional life is always a "projection" of your personal life. How you do anything is how to you do everything.
@AlexMandossian

_____

_____

_____

125

Happiness in your personal and professional life is "getting" what you want AND "wanting" what you get.
@AlexMandossian

_____

_____

_____

126

Having "Hope" in business is not about KNOW-ING how to get from Point A to Point B; it's simply knowing there IS a Point B.
@AlexMandossian

_____

_____

_____

127

You can't be 100% committed to great new ideas
sometimes.
@AlexMandossian

128

What your "outer voice" resists, your "inner voice"
persists.
@AlexMandossian

129

Discipline isn't meant to be hard. It's the label we attach to the annoying feeling when learning a new success habit.
@AlexMandossian

_____

_____

_____

130

Multitaskers are suckers for task irrelevance, because they are mediocre at everything and masters of nothing.
@AlexMandossian

_____

_____

_____

131

Business owners can learn much from studying turtles - they make progress only when they stick their neck out.
@AlexMandossian

_____

_____

_____

132

The truly genuine "Social Influencer" is not a "sage from stage;" they are a "guide from the side."
@AlexMandossian

_____

_____

_____

133

Beware of quitting "too soon." Dr. Seuss was rejected by 23 publishers, but the 24th publisher sold over six million books.
@AlexMandossian

_____

_____

_____

134

Nothing is as persuasive as the truth in business and in life.
@AlexMandossian

_____

_____

_____

135

Remember: the ripest fruits are typically the hard- est to reach high on the tree. @AlexMandossian

_____

_____

_____

136

Don't stress over not achieving your goals you set that are too high. Get worried about achieving goals that were set too low. @AlexMandossian

_____

_____

_____

137

A very wise entrepreneurial mentor once said,
"The light at the end of the tunnel is not a light,
it's a mirror."
@AlexMandossian

_____

_____

_____

138

Great business minds are like parachutes: they
must be opened in order to work properly.
@AlexMandossian

_____

_____

_____

139

The velocity of decision -making causes more permanent and positive change than the quality ofdecision-making.
@AlexMandossian

_____

_____

_____

140

Remember, you're never as good as you think you are - you're better!
@AlexMandossian

_____

_____

_____

Take the 4-minute Serial Entrepreneur Assessment at
MarketingOnlineFunnel.com

Acknowledgement

It's remarkable that this is my first book.

After over twenty-five years of teaching and training other serial entrepreneurs on how to get more exposure and visibility and accelerate the growth of their businesses, this is my first book. After being hired to personally consult more than ninety authors to make their books international best-sellers, this is my first book! I'm finally "eating my own cooking," as my good friend and colleague, Keith Cunningham, says.

As I sat down to write this Acknowledgments section, I knew then as I still know now, that I'm leaving hundreds of people out who deserve recognition for my progress and success. It's impossible to thank everyone who impacted the development of this book. So if you don't see your name listed below, I apologize to you in advance and I hope you reach out so I can thank you personally.

As I said in the opening page, this book is dedicated to the Serial Entrepreneur who wants to live with more honor by becoming the person they pretend to be. I do owe the great Socrates a quick "Thank You," because that dedication was me "repurposing" a favorite quote of his.

To my mother, Carol, and my father, George . . . thank you for making a decision about forty weeks before March 9, 1964 for putting me "in play" for the game of life. I played to win and I won the ovarian lottery! To my sister, Taleen, who with her husband, Arthur, made a decision to bring my niece, Grace, and nephew, Alex (named after me!), into the world.

I've heard it said that a child is the Universe's opinion that "life should go onward and upward," so I would be remiss if I didn't appreciate my former wife, Aimee, with whom I share our two children, Gabriel and Breanna. I can say with a clear conscience that I've learned more from my nuclear family than the rest of my teachers and students combined!

Useful Life Lessons from a Recovering Serial Entrepreneur

To my life-partner, Sandra Bravo, who is like the rudder of my ship that sets sail each day to explore new territories of understanding , personally and professionally. Thank you again, Sandra, I love you.

To my Team for whom I can never appreciate enough : Sandra Bravo, Lio Fernandez , Michelle Bassett , Aditya Jagannatha , Souvit Singharoy , Jon Marino , Jessica Dean , Jake Larson , Diana Blanco , Jennifer Glick , Riccardo Romano , Lloyd Minthorne , and so many others who could fill dozens of more pages!

To past team members and countless volunteers who assisted me with virtual and physical events. To my strategic alliance partners from whom I learn daily: Eben Pagan, Justin Livingston, Ryan Deiss, Berny Dohrmann, Lisa Sasevich, Vishen Lakhiani, Bill Baren, Jack Canfield, Patty Aubery, Milana Leshinsky, Joe Polish, Blue Melnick, Bari Baumgardner, Paul Colligan, Mike Filsaime, Jeff Walker, Brendon Burchard, Ted Prodromou, Ian Marsh, Christian Mickelsen, David Perdew, Joe Polish, Mike Koenigs, Bill and Steve Harrison, Scott Martineau, Armand Morin, Steven Olsher, and the list could go on and on for another hundred pages!

To my three most important mentors: T. Harv Eker, Roy H. Williams, and Ivan Misner. To Roland Frasier, who wrote the Afterword of this book and distracted me long enough to compile and curate the Alexisms you've just read. I am in Mitchell's debt for openly and decisively bringing me into the "Aha" family of published authors.

And finally, I write these words to appreciate you, the reader. Without you, the contents of this book would be far less relevant to the world, because all 140+ Alexisms would still be in my head. I hope our paths cross often and I hope you keep up with the social conversation on our Facebook Community at <u>www.MarketingOnlineFunnel.com/MVPgroup</u>.

About the Author

Since 1993, Alex Mandossian has generated over $400 million insales and profitsfor his students , clients , and partners on five continents . He is the Founder of MarketingOnlineFunnel .com , and his enrollment strategies helped transform his annual income in 2001 into amonthly income by 2003, and eventually into anhourly income by 2006 . By 2007 , his proven online marketing strategies generated $1.2 millioninlessthantwenty-nineminutesduringonemagicalproductlaunch.

Alexisacknowledged byhiscolleagues asthe"Warren Bufetofthe Internet" because ofhisuniqueabilitytomakemoneyforhisstudents andjointventure partners. Hehas shared the stage with diverse leaders such as Sir Richard Branson , Harvey Mackay , Donald Trump , Tony Robbins , Robert Kiyosaki , Suze Orman , Mikhail Gorbachev , andHisHolinesstheDalaiLama.

Asa Master"VirtualPresenter"with over22,000 hours ofonlinetrainingtime,Alex's lifetime goal (with hiscolleague, Jack Canfield) istoinfluence over onemillion other trainersbyhis77thbirthday.

To contact Alex Mandossian, please email Support@MarketingOnlineFunnel.com, or mailto

Heritage House International, Inc.530

Alameda del Prado, Suite 399 Novato, CA 94949

Take the 4-minute Serial Entrepreneur Assessment at
MarketingOnlineFunnel.com

Printed in the USA
CPSIA information can be obtained
at www.ICGtesting.com
LVHW010327311223
767805LV00006B/270